D0098735

Code of the Samurai

A Modern Translation of the
Bushido Shoshinsu

Code of the Samurai

A Modern Translation of the
Bushido Shoshinsu

Thomas Cleary
Illustrated by Oscar Ratti

TUTTLE Publishing

Tokyo │ Rutland, Vermont │ Singapore

Published by Tuttle Publishing, an imprint of Periplus Editions (HK) Ltd.

www.tuttlepublishing.com

Copyright © 1999 by Thomas Cleary

All rights reserved. No part of this publication may be reproduced or utilized in any form or by any means, electronic or mechanical, including photocopying, recording, or by any information storage and retrieval system, without prior written permission from the publisher

Library of Congress Cataloging-in-Publication Data

Daidoji, Yuzan 1639-1730
(Budo shoshinshu. English)
(The code of the samurai: a modern translation of the Bushido shoshinshu /
Thomas Cleary ; illustrated by Oscar Ratti.
xvii, 98 p. : ill. ; 20 cm.
1. Bushido. 2. Samurai—Conduct of Life. I Cleary, Thomas F., 1949-. II. Title.
BJ971B8D313 1999   98052721
170/.44/0952—dc21   CIP

ISBN 978-0-8048-3190-1

Distributed by

North America, Latin America & Europe
Tuttle Publishing
364 Innovation Drive, North Clarendon, VT 05759-9436 U.S.A.
Tel: 1 (802) 773-8930 | Fax: 1 (802) 773-6993
info@tuttlepublishing.com | www.tuttlepublishing.com

Japan
Tuttle Publishing
Yaekari Building, 3rd Floor, 5-4-12 Osaki, Shinagawa-ku, Tokyo 141 0032
Tel: (81) 3 5437-017 | Fax: (81) 3 5437-0755
sales@tuttle.co.jp | www.tuttle.co.jp

Asia Pacific
Berkeley Books Pte. Ltd.
3 Kallang Sector #04-01/02, Singapore 349278
Tel: (65) 6280-1330 | Fax: (65) 6280-6290
inquiries@periplus.com.sg | www.periplus.com

22 21 20 19 18   23 22 21 20 19   1811CM
Printed in China

TUTTLE PUBLISHING® is a registered trademark of Tuttle Publishing,
a division of Periplus Editions (HK) Ltd.

Contents

PART III

Introduction

J APANESE   CULTURE   IS often considered unique, both by foreign visitors and observers and by the Japanese people themselves. This uniqueness is sometimes attributed to Japan's geographical situation as an island nation, separated as it is from continental Asia by unusually dangerous waters. The policy of *sakoku*, or national isolation, adopted by the shoguns from 1639 to 1854, is also generally considered to have contributed to Japanese cultural insularity; it also helps to explain particular Japanese attitudes toward foreign peoples.

In many respects, whether at home or interacting with outsiders, one of the most powerful cumulative and residual influences of history on the Japanese culture and mentality, even to the present day, has been the extraordinarily long duration of military rule in Japan. The entrenchment of the samurai as the dominant class had profound cultural and psychological effects on the Japanese people. These effects were brought about by the acute changes in society that martial rule effected by *force majeure*, and also by chronic indoctrination of society subsequently promulgated by the military governments to legitimize their rule ideologically.

The samurai class originated as an offshoot or special-ization of the aristocracy. Generally speaking, a polygamous upper class normally produced more children than could be absorbed at the same level of society. The rule of primo-geniture, furthermore, meant that only one son inherited the full privileges of his father. These factors created natural and social pressures toward differentiation in the career patterns of the scions of the upper classes.

In Japan, as in Europe and elsewhere, those sons of aris-tocratic fathers who did not inherit their paternal estate com-monly became warriors or monastics. In Japan both of these specializations were originally conceived for the protection of the state; the ancient warriors were first called *samurai* or "attendants" because they formed the armed guard of the aristocracy. When the samurai eventually took the reins of government from the aristocracy, as an independent class, one way in which they manifested their new status and dig-nity was to distance themselves from the "attendant" samu-rai label and call themselves *bushi*, "warriors" or "knights."

The ascendancy of the warrior class in Japan was fore-shadowed by its solidification and empowerment, over gen-erations of expansionist wars against the Ainu people, who inhabited Honshu, the main island of Japan, before the mod-ern Japanese settled there. The earlier inhabitants of Kyushu, the southern island of Japan, which seems to have been the main route of ancestral Sino-Korean/Japanese entry into the islands, had been decimated and absorbed comparatively early on in the course of the Japanese settlement. The Ainu of the main island, however, a bear-hunting people, stoutly resisted the expansion of the Japanese for a remarkably long time. The Japanese warrior clans who opposed the Ainu and settled the eastern frontiers thus developed into a stern and hardy breed.

Eventually the Ainu were driven up into Hokkaido, the northernmost of the main islands of modern Japan, leaving the Japanese warrior clans with effective power in eastern Japan. They still exercised this power in the name of the central government, however, as did the warriors in other parts of Japan who administered and policed the outlying lands owned by the increasingly urbanized aristocracy. Once the Ainu had been vanquished from the main island and a degree of national security had been realized, the warrior class and the aristocracy grew further apart in occupational outlook, as the aristocracy focused on cultural development while the warriors handled military and administrative affairs.

Over time the excesses of aristocratic self-indulgence, well documented in parodies of the times, resulted in a certain degree of enervation. At the same time, the responsibilities of the warriors made such demands on them that they in turn demanded a greater share in the revenue from the lands they administered on behalf of the urban aristocracy. These circumstances eventually led to cession of lands to warrior clans, as the most direct form of revenue sharing. Ultimately the land and power held by warrior clans throughout the provinces made possible the establishment of a national military government, operating in parallel with the civil government, which still administered imperial and aristocratic holdings, but more powerful and able to domineer over the latter.

The first military government of Japan, the *Bakufu*, or Tent Government, was established in 1186 in Kamakura, a mountain fastness not far from what is now Tokyo in eastern Japan. This was to be the first of three Tent Governments that ruled Japan from that time until 1868, a period of nearly seven hundred years.

The stability of the Kamakura regime was fatally rocked by Mongol invasions in 1274 and 1281. Although samurai resistance and storms prevented a Mongol victory, the costs of the campaigns weakened the Japanese military government. In a feudal system such as it was, rewards for military service were customarily given in the form of land grants from expropriated territories. In fending off a foreign invasion, however, no new lands were taken, and there was nothing to plunder, so warriors could not be paid for their services in those forms. Resulting dissatisfaction among the knightly clans who had defended Japan against the Mongol invaders fatally destabilized the regime of the Tent Government of Kamakura, and it finally collapsed in 1333.

After a period of civil strife, a new military regime was established in 1336 under the leadership of Ashikaga Takauji. The new Tent Government was established in the Muromachi district of Kyoto, the ancient imperial capital, and took a greater interest in the culture and politics of the old aristocracy. For the first fifty years of the new military regime, the imperial house itself was divided into rival factions, and the tension and political instability this produced were exacerbated by the incompleteness of the Ashikaga network of alliances among the warrior clans. A major civil war broke out in 1467, after which political stability was not to be restored for over a hundred years. The century of Japanese history following this civil war is called the Era of the Warring States, a more or less continuous series of contests for dominion among warlord factions.

The last Ashikaga shogun was finally deposed in 1574 by Oda Nobunaga, the first of a series of three warlords who finally unified Japan under military rule. Oda was followed by Toyotomi Hideyoshi, and he by Tokugawa Ieyasu, who established the third Tent Government in 1603. Set up in the new city of Edo, modern Tokyo, not far from the old military capital of Kamakura, the Tokugawa regime subsequently shut Japan off from the outside world and maintained its own system of samurai rule for more than 250 years, until 1867.

The Tokugawa regime was more tightly organized than previous military governments, with greater political and social controls. The century of civil wars is characterized by Japanese historians as a time of *gekokujo*, or "those below overcoming those above." Many of the warlords who emerged during this era were of a new breed, risen from the lower ranks, even from the peasantry. Tokugawa Ieyasu was himself of humbler origins, and when he had established himself as the first shogun of the new Tent Government in Edo, his government instituted measures to prevent any further social change or mobility.

One of the most telling moves of the Tokugawa regime was to transform the class system into a caste system. Japanese society had always been hierarchical, but personal and family fortunes rose and fell over the generations. Under the new system, the four main classes of warrior, farmer, artisan, and merchant were legally fixed as hereditary castes, whose lifestyles were defined by specific sumptuary laws for each caste. Below these four castes were two classes of outcasts, called the Polluted Ones and the Inhumans. Although wealthy merchants were able to secure marital and adoptive alliances with warrior families, and free people could be outcast for crimes, in general the four castes were kept distinctly separated.

Another major innovation of the Tokugawa military regime was the removal of the samurai from the land. Under the earlier feudal systems, a warlord paid his vassals in land grants, from which they would extract a portion of the revenue for their upkeep. The Tokugawa system was designed to undermine the possibility of formation of independent warrior bands in the provinces by having the samurai live in the precincts of the castle towns of their lords and receive their stipends in rice, rather than live directly on the land in the countryside.

This organizational device provided for greater control of the warrior caste as a whole by the central military government, and also transformed the samurai more extensively than ever into an administrative class. To compensate psychologically for the urbanization and bureaucratization of the warrior class, martial arts were developed into highly theatrical, philosophically elaborated systems of mental and moral training.

Samurai also became scholars and physicians. The humbler ones who did not work for big houses often eked out a living teaching Confucian classics to children in primary schools or home tutoring. A great many of the sons of poorer samurai families went into religious orders, particular the Rinzai order of Zen Buddhism. Some of the new breed of scholars of the Tokugawa era even reinterpreted Shinto, the ancient religion, and laid the foundation for modern Japanese imperialism.

The samurai warrior caste therefore exerted great influence on the whole of Japanese society, not only through its role as ruler and law giver, but also through its patterns of patronage, such as the cultural and educational activities of its noncombatants and clients. As a process of many hundreds of years' duration, this element of Japanese civilization acquired extraordinary momentum and force, both politically and psychologically. Even today the conventional Japanese culture and mentality cannot be understood without recognizing the residual influence of those samurai centuries.

The last challenge to the Tokugawa regime was a Christian rebellion crushed in 1636. After that, Christianity was outlawed and Japan was isolated from foreign contact, except for one trade ship a year from China and one from Holland. With civil war ended and Western imperialism excluded, Japan flourished within the rigid structures of its feudal way of life, acquiring a level of national discipline that would enable it to adapt to the modern world with greater rapidity than other Asian nations.

An irony of the Pax Tokugawa for the samurai class was that with the end of chronic warfare and the enjoyment of material prosperity, the elders perceived a weakening of the warrior spirit. Having inherited a martial tradition in which the rulers themselves were warriors, the elders could only interpret the decline of knighthood as a threat to moral and social order. Thus the codification of traditional practical philosophies was made a part of the cultural norm of the Tokugawa period.

The Code of the Samurai, whose Japanese title, *Bushido Shoshinshu,* means *Bushido for Beginners,* was written for novice knights of the new era. Its author, Taira Shigesuke, a Confucian scholar and military scientist, was born in 1639, the year after implementation of the national isolation policy, and died in 1730, having lived through the peak of Pax Tokugawa prosperity. This handbook, written after five hundred years of military rule in Japan, was composed to provide practical and moral instruction for warriors, correcting wayward tendencies and outlining the personal, social, and professional standards of conduct characteristic of Bushido, or the way of the warrior, the Japanese chivalric tradition.

In the modern day, much of the cultural isolation that exists around the world is due to misinformation and misunderstanding. *The Code of the Samurai* presents a remarkably faithful mirror of many of the characteristics and habits of modern-day Japanese civilization, representing as it does a core tradition of longstanding prestige and power. Personal responsibilities, familial relations, public duties, education, finance, ethics, and so on—all these aspects of life and more are treated in this text from the point of view of the martial spirit of Japanese knighthood. Even the forms of professional and political incompetence and corruption with which Japan struggles today are described with uncanny accuracy in this 300-year-old book, so deeply did the feudal and military modes of rule that spawned them strike roots in Japanese society. This handbook is thus an essential resource for all who wish to understand Japan and the Japanese people realistically.

PART ONE

General Discussion

ONE WHO IS SUPPOSED to be a warrior considers it his foremost concern to keep death in mind at all times, every day and every night, from the morning of New Year's Day through the night of New Year's Eve.

As long as you keep death in mind at all times, you will also fulfill the ways of loyalty and familial duty. You will also avoid myriad evils and calamities, you will be physically sound and healthy, and you will live a long life. What is more, your character will improve and your virtue will grow.

Here are the reasons for that. All human life is likened to evening dew and morning frost, considered something quite fragile and ephemeral. While this is so of all people's lives, the life of the warrior is particularly precarious.

If people comfort their minds with the assumption that they will live a long time, something might happen, because they think they will have forever to do their work and look after their parents—they may fail to perform for their employers and also treat their parents thoughtlessly.

But if you realize that the life that is here today is not certain on the morrow, then when you take your orders from your employer, and when you look in on your parents, you will have the sense that this may be the last time—so you cannot fail to become truly attentive to your employer and your parents. This is why I say you also fulfill the paths of loyalty and familial duty when you keep death in mind.

In any case, when you forget death and become inattentive, you are not circumspect about things. You may say something offensive to someone and get into an argument. You may challenge something you might as well have ignored, and get into a quarrel.

Or you may stroll about in resorts where you have no business, not avoiding the crowds, where you might bump into some oaf and get into an unexpected brawl. You could lose your own life, get your employer bad publicity, and cause your parents and siblings difficulties.

All this trouble comes from inattentiveness when you fail to keep death in mind at all times.

When you always keep death in mind, when you speak and when you reply to what others say, you understand the weight and significance of every word as a warrior by profession, so you do not engage in futile arguments. As a matter of course you do not go to dubious places even if people invite you, so there is no way for you to get into unexpected predicaments. This is why I say you will avoid myriad evils and calamities if you keep death in mind.

People of all social classes, high and low, constantly overeat, drink too much, and indulge in their desires to an unhealthy degree, all because of forgetting about death. This puts a strain on their internal organs, so they may die remarkably young, or else become sickly or invalid.

When you always keep death in mind, even if you are

young and healthy, you already know how to take care of yourself. You moderate food and drink, avoid sexual addiction, and behave prudently. As a result, you are physically sound. Because you are healthy, you will live a long time.

When you assume that your stay in this world will last, various wishes occur to you, and you become very desirous. You want what others have, and cling to your own possessions, developing a mercantile mentality.

When you always keep death in mind, covetousness naturally weakens, and to that degree a grabby, greedy attitude logically does not occur. That is why I say your character improves.

Yet there is the question of how to keep death in mind.

To just keep sitting there all the time waiting for death twenty-four hours a day, like the monk Shinkai of whom Yoshida no Kenkō wrote in his *Tsurezuregusa*, might be appropriate for monks' training, but it is not in accord with the aim of martial training. If you face death in that way, loyalty and familial duty to your employer and parents will be neglected, and your professional warriorhood will wind up defective. That will never do.

The idea is to take care of your public and private duties day and night, and then whenever you have any free time when your mind is unoccupied, you think of death, bringing it to mind attentively. It is said that in the great hero Kusunoki Masashige's instructions to his son Masayuki, he told him to "always get used to death."

This is for the understanding of neophyte knights.

Education

WARRIORS STAND IN a position above the other three castes, and are supposed to be professional administrators, so they need to study and gain an extensive understanding of the principles of things.

Even so, warriors in times of warfare invariably participate in their first combat by the age of fifteen or sixteen, doing their work as knights, so they practice martial arts from the age of twelve or thirteen. For that reason they have no time for study, and are naturally illiterate.

During the Era of the Civil Wars, there were any number of warriors who couldn't even look up a word in the dictionary. That was not necessarily because of their own negligence, or because their parents raised them badly, but because their immediate need was to concentrate on military arts.

As for warriors born in the present era, when the land is at peace, I wouldn't say it doesn't matter if they care little for military arts, but since this is not a world in which they absolutely must go into combat from the age of fifteen or sixteen, they should be taught classical literature, reading, and writing, from the age of seven or eight. Then when they are fifteen or sixteen, they ought to be taught to practice archery, horsemanship, and all the other martial arts. This should be the basic aim of educating the children of warriors in peaceful times.

Illiteracy among warriors in times of chronic warfare has a reason. There is no legitimate reason for illiteracy among warriors in an era of peace. Children are not to blame for this; it is only due to the negligence and irresponsibility of the parents. Ultimately, it is because they do not know the way to love their children.

Familial Duty

F OR WARRIORS, TAKING good care of parents is fundamental. If people do not care for their parents, they are not good, even if they are exceptionally smart, well-spoken, and handsome.

Let me explain. In the way of the warrior, it is essential to do it right from root to branch. If you do not understand the root and the branch, there is no way for you to know your duty. One who does not know his duty can hardly be called a warrior.

Knowing the root and the branch means understanding that our parents are the root of our bodies, and our bodies are branches of the flesh and bones of our parents. It is because of the desire to establish ourselves, who are the branches, that circumstances arise whereby we neglect our parents, who are the roots. This is because of failure to understand root and branch.

Now then, there are two ways of taking good care of your parents.

Suppose there are parents of a mild temperament, who educate their children with true kindness and affection, provide for them, marry them well, and then retire, leaving them well situated, with an adequate estate. For children of such parents to take ordinary care of them is nothing particularly praiseworthy or impressive.

Even with strangers, when they have treated us kindly and helped us out personally or financially, we do not overlook it—if they are in need, we are even willing to set aside our own affairs. How much less could we ever expect to think that we have done enough to care for our parents, considering the depth of the love they have shown us in every way! For this reason I say that ordinary familial duty is nothing remarkable.

Now suppose there are parents who are obstreperous, cranky, and argumentative, who insist on running the household and refuse to hand over anything, who are importunate, inconsiderate, and demanding, and on top of that complain to others how vexed and troubled they are by the poor treatment they get from their sons, thus damaging their children's reputations. To honor even such unreasonable parents as parents, to take the trouble to humor them, to lament their aging and decline, and take care of them sincerely, without a bit of negligence—this is the aim of dutiful children.

When a warrior with this spirit takes an overlord as an employer and becomes an official, he understands the requirements of loyalty and duty. When his employer is flourishing this is a matter of course, but even when something unexpected happens to his employer and he has all sorts of troubles, a warrior is still fiercely loyal and does not leave his employer's side even when a hundred allies are reduced to ten, even when ten are reduced to one, so steadfastly loyal in battle as to disregard his own life.

Parents and employers, familial duty and loyalty—these differ only in name, for there is no difference in the sincerity of the heart. So it is that an ancient is reported to have said, "Look for loyal ministers in homes with filial sons." There is no such thing as someone who is disrespectful to his parents yet faithful to his employer. If someone is so immature as to be remiss in familial care for his parents, who are the origin of his own body, there is no way he can be moved by the kindness of an employer, who is not his flesh and blood, to be completely loyal.

If a man who is not caring toward his parents at home does go into the service of a lord, he keeps his eyes on his employer's balance sheet, and as soon as he sees any little slip his attitude changes; in an emergency he will flee or turn traitor. There are cases like this past and present; this is something to be ashamed of, something to be wary of.

Principles of Warriors

I N   T H E   C O D E   O F warriors there are two kinds of principles, with four levels.

The two kinds of principles are ordinary principles and emergency principles. The ordinary principles include principles of knighthood and principles of weaponry. The emergency principles include army principles and combat principles.

The principles of knighthood include washing your hands and feet and bathing morning and night, keeping your body clean, shaving and dressing your hair every morning, dressing formally according to the season and circumstances, and always keeping your fan in your belt, not to mention your long and short swords. When dealing with guests, you treat them courteously according to their status, and avoid useless talk. Even when you partake of a bowl of rice or a cup of tea, you are always careful not to be slovenly.

If you are in public service, when off duty you do not simply lounge around; you read, practice calligraphy, contemplate ancient stories or ancient warrior codes. Whether you are walking, standing still, sitting down, or reclining, in your conduct and manner you carry yourself in a way that exemplifies a genuine warrior.

As for the principles of weaponry, the first thing to learn is swordsmanship, then lancing, riding, archery, shooting, and any other martial arts. Your duty is to study, practice, and master them, so you can be ever ready with them.

Once you have cultivated these two levels, the principles of knighthood and the principles of weaponry, you lack nothing in the way of ordinary principles. In the eyes of ordinary people you will seem like a good warrior, worthy of employ. However, warriors are fundamentally emergency men. When there is a civil disturbance, they set aside their usual knightly ways for the moment, adopt military terminology for their superiors, comrades, and subordinates, doff their formal suits and put on armor, take up weapons, and head for the enemy's ground. There are all sorts of manners and forms of doing this, collectively referred to as army principles. It is imperative to know these.

Next are combat principles. When your enemies and allies clash in battle, if your dispositions and maneuvers work as planned, you gain victory; otherwise, you lose the advantage and suffer defeat. There are traditional secrets to these various maneuvers and dispositions; these are called combat principles. It is imperative to know them.

Army principles and combat principles are the two levels of emergency principles.

A warrior who has cultivated the four levels of ordinary and emergency principles to perfection is considered a top-class knight. If you have accomplished the two levels of ordinary principles, you are competent for service as a knight, but if you have not mastered the two levels of emergency principles, you cannot be a samurai commander, a group leader, a magistrate, or anything like that.

Accordingly, making this distinction, to become an all-around warrior it is essential to practice the principles of knighthood and weaponry, as well as the inner secrets of army and combat principles, determining never to give up without having become a top-class knight.

Not Forgetting Combat

For warriors it is essential to keep the spirit of combat in mind twenty-four hours a day, whether walking, standing still, sitting down, or reclining, never forgetting it.

Japanese custom is different from that of other countries in that even lower-class people such as farmers, merchants, and artisans all treasure a rusty short sword. This is a Japanese custom, but even so, these three lower castes do not make soldiery a profession.

In warrior houses, even the underlings and squires always wear a short sword, as a rule; how much more so is it imperative for full-fledged knights to see to it that they are never without swords at their sides, even for a moment. For this reason, really serious warriors even wear an edgeless sword or a wooden sword to the bath.

If you are this attentive even at home, how much the more so when you go out. It is not impossible that on the road, or at your destination, you may run into someone in a drunken rage, or some kind of fool, and get into an unexpected duel. There is an old saying, "When you go out your door, it is like seeing an enemy." Since you are a professional warrior and wear swords at your side, you should never forget the spirit of combat at any time.

When you do not forget the spirit of combat, you also spontaneously act in accordance with the reality of keeping death in mind.

A warrior who wears two swords at his side but does not put the spirit of combat into his heart is nothing but a peasant or a merchant wearing the skin of a warrior.

Monk-Warriors

S INCE ANCIENT TIMES there has been a tradition of monk-warrior, and there are indeed similarities between monks and warriors.

For example, in the Zen schools, the ones called Librarian and Assembly Leader are all common monks, similar in status to the rank-and-file warriors in peripheral services.

On the next level of monastics are the officers and assistant teachers, who correspond to military officers like the groups leaders of the knights of a domain, or the chiefs of the foot soldiers.

Now then, even though they are still renunciants, when monks put on colorful religious vestments, hold symbols of authority in their hands, and lead large groups, they are called Elders or Masters. They correspond to the warriors who have their own flags, insignia, and batons of authority, the commanders of knights or infantry, who lead troops and command armies, or the commanders of archers.

However, when it comes to the pursuit of learning, the way the warrior bands do it seems far inferior to the way the Buddhist brethren do it. To explain this in some detail, the Buddhist way is that while one is a common monk one leaves one's teacher's side to visit many monasteries and mountains and meet numerous learned masters and enlightened guides, and accumulate achievements in Zen study and attainment; even if one rises through the ranks of officers and assistant teacher, or becomes an Elder or Master, even if one assumes the abbacy of a main temple or monastery, one still pursues learning to its ultimate end without the slightest embarrassment, waiting for the time to become a public teacher to arrive.

It would be desirable for things to be like this among warriors, but even common warriors without offices, working in outside service, are salaried even when idle. Since they do not lack for food, clothing, or housing, even the young ones have wives and children. They make it their business to nap morning and afternoon, and do not study or work on the military arts that are norms for warriors, much less concentrate on the more remote matters of army principles and combat principles.

Frittering each day away, as they pass the months and years, their hair goes gray and they start balding. Since they seem to be of appropriate age, they are given emeritus status. If, for example, they become emissaries, they set right out immediately and somehow get the job done, with the help of colleagues, but when there is an unusual mission to a distant province they are taken aback and filled with anxiety. Even as they are preparing for the journey they get professional advice from predecessors and borrow traditional manuals of protocol; if they eventually get the job done, that is called getting off lucky. We cannot say that this is the way things should be in this profession.

To explain this in some detail, the official duties of the warrior caste are generally well defined, so you should learn about them while you have no office yourself. Whenever you meet able and experienced officers present at a gathering, leave off useless conversation and inquire into such things that occur to you as might be useful tips for the future. Question repeatedly, listen carefully, and remember everything. Borrow old manuals of procedure and protocol, even illustrations, and make copies of these for future reference. Thus if you absorb the general outlines of the duties of the various offices, then whatever office you may assume at any time it should be easy for you to perform.

Furthermore, learning how to do things thanks to seniors and colleagues, and getting things done with their help, is the manner of times of normalcy. In the event of a crisis, in contrast, since you cannot avail yourself of the assistance and guidance of others, there is no alternative but to resolve things by your own individual judgment, for good or for bad.

As an example, a military inspector has to know the numbers of enemy troops, the quality of their battle formations and preparations, the security of castles, the advantages of terrain, and the prospects of victory in battle. For this reason, the office of military inspector has traditionally been considered a difficult one. However, if there is some mistake in one's perceptions as military inspector, it is mostly attributed to individual misjudgment. When it comes to the ranks of infantry commander and above, with the authority to command, the life and death of the troops depend on them; so to disgrace the warrior band by incompetent arrogation of leadership is the ultimate outrage.

This is like a Zen monk who neglects to study the doctrines of the religion while a common monk, but eventually becomes an Elder or Master simply because he is getting old and going bald, donning colorful robes, wielding a symbol of authority, and leading a large group.

However, when a charlatan like this does something disgraceful in front of a serious audience, he becomes a laughingstock to the whole crowd; he alone is shamed, and can only withdraw—there is no danger to the community. In contrast to this, when a warrior in a commanding role makes a blunder in leadership, that endangers the lives of his troops, causing great harm.

It is important to understand this, and consequently use your free time out of office to perfect your cultivation of army principles and combat principles. Study and practice so that there is no office you cannot perform, even the position of command.

Right and Wrong

AS LONG AS IT IS realized and accepted that warriors must comprehend right and wrong, and strive to do right and avoid wrong, then the way of warriors is alive.

Right and wrong mean good and evil. Right is good, wrong is evil. Ordinarily people are not totally devoid of understanding of good and evil, right and wrong, but they find it boring and tiresome to act rightly and strive for goodness. Acting wrongly and behaving badly is fun and familiar, so they drift toward things that are wrong and bad, and it becomes tiresome for them to do right and foster good.

The complete moron who cannot distinguish good and bad or right and wrong is not even worth talking about. Once you have determined something to be wrong and bad, to avoid demands and justice and do what is wrong is not the attitude of a knight. That is the epitome of the immaturity of modern times. Its origin might be attributed to lack of endurance in people. Lack of endurance sounds all right, but you will find that it comes from cowardice.

Therefore warriors consider it essential to always beware of wrong and pursue right.

Now then, there are three ways of doing right.

Suppose you are going somewhere with an acquaintance who has a hundred ounces of gold and wants to leave it at your house until returning, instead of taking the trouble to carry it with him. Suppose you take the gold and put it away where no one can find it. Now suppose your companion dies during the trip, perhaps from food poisoning or stroke. No one else knows he left gold at your house, and no one else knows you have it.

Under these circumstances, if you have no thought but of sorrow for the tragedy, and you report the gold to the relatives of the deceased, sending it to them as soon as possible, then you can truly be said to have done right.

Now suppose the man with the gold was just an acquaintance, not such a close friend. No one knows about the gold he left with you, so there will be no inquiries. You happen to be in tight circumstances at the moment, so this is a bit of luck; why not just keep quiet about it?

If you are ashamed to find such thoughts occurring to you, and so you change your mind and return the gold to the rightful heirs, you could be said to have done right out of a sense of shame.

Now suppose someone in your household—maybe your wife, your children, or your servants—knows about the gold. Suppose you return the gold to the legitimate heirs out of shame for any designs anyone in your household might conceive, and out of fear for the legal consequences. Then you should be said to do right out of shame in relation to others.

But what would you do if no one knew about it at all?

Even in such a case, it could still hardly be said you were not a man who knows what is right and does it.

The process of cultivating the practice of doing right begins with fear of being disrespected by those close to you, starting with your family and servants, then advances to refraining from doing wrong and deliberately doing right for fear of incurring the shame of being censured and ridiculed by society at large. If you do this, it will naturally become habitual, so eventually you develop a mentality that prefers to follow what is right and disdains to do wrong.

In the context of martial valor, furthermore, those who are born brave are not fazed by arrow and gunfire on the battlefield, however intense it may be; they make targets of their bodies, pinned between loyalty and duty. The courage of their forward-marching spirit also shows physically, so it goes without saying that they are splendid in action.

There are also those who are hesitant in danger, their hearts pounding and their knees trembling, yet they go ahead, along with the brave ones, realizing that their comrades will see if they alone do not go, determined not to expose themselves to ridicule later on. Although they are far inferior to the naturally brave ones, when they have gone through this time and again, fighting in battle after battle until they get used to it, eventually their minds settle and they become praiseworthy knights, strong and firm, not so different from those who are naturally brave.

So when it comes to doing right and being courageous, there is nothing to go on but a sense of shame. If you do wrong, unconcerned that people will say it is wrong, or if you are cowardly without caring that people will laugh at you for spinelessness, there is nothing anyone can teach you.

The Valiant

O N   T H E   W A R R I O R ' S
path, only three things
are considered essential: loyalty, duty, and valor. We speak
of knights who work loyally, knights who are faithful to duty,
and knights who are courageous and strong. Warriors who
combine these three virtues of loyalty, duty, and valor in one
person are considered the knights of the highest order.

Knights of the highest order are rare, even in a group
of a hundred or a thousand warriors. As for the distinction
between knights who are loyal workers and knights who are
faithful to duty, this constantly shows in their conduct and is
easily discerned.

It may be wondered whether the duty of a valorous
man might be impossible to know in an era of peace like the
present, when there is no war going on. That is not so, as I
will explain.

Generally speaking, courage is not something that only
appears when you put on armor, take up weapons, and fight
in combat. The difference between the courageous and the
cowardly can be seen in everyday life.

One who is naturally valorous exercises loyalty and
devotion to his employer and parents, and if he has any free

time he studies literature and keeps up the practice of martial arts. He avoids personal luxury, and disdains to waste even a penny. He is not stingy, however, and spends his money freely when necessary.

Anywhere forbidden by the regulations of his employment, or disliked by his parents, he will avoid going even if he wants to. He will give up even those things that are hard to give up, just to avoid displeasing his employer and parents.

He keeps fit, and because he wants to accomplish something significant in life he always takes care of his health, moderating his diet and avoiding drink. He also keeps warily aloof from sexual feelings, the foremost confusion of humankind, and he has a patient, tolerant attitude in respect to everything else.

All of these reflect the mentality of the courageous.

As for the cowardly, they merely feign respect for employers and parents superficially, without really caring for them. They do not avoid things forbidden by employers or disliked by parents; they even frequent places they should not go, and do things they should not do. Acting as they please, they habitually nap mornings and afternoons. They hate literary studies, and even if they practice martial arts they do not pursue any of them seriously. They just talk boastfully about skills they cannot really perform.

They are spendthrifts when it comes to useless crazes and fancy dining, but extremely stingy when it comes to necessities. They give no thought to the maintenance of the heirlooms they have inherited from their parents, much less to the replacement of other military equipment.

If they are sickly, they cannot enter active public service; mindless of the worry they cause their parents, they overeat, drink too much, and become addicted to sex.

Wearing away yourself and your life like this is something that comes from a weak and immature mind unable to endure and tolerate things. This generally reflects the mentality of a cowardly knight.

Therefore I say that the courageous and the cowardly can certainly be distinguished in everyday life.

Courtesy and Respect

THE TWO PATHS OF loyalty and familial duty are not only obligatory for warriors; farmers, artisans, and merchants are not different in this respect.

Nevertheless, when young people or servants are unmannerly in conversation and other interaction with their employers or parents, and yet this is overlooked as long as they are sincere in their regard for their employers and parents, this is the loyalty and familial duty of the lower three classes. In the way of warriors, no matter how much you may treasure loyalty and familial duty in your heart, without the courteous manners to express respect for your employers and honor for your parents, you cannot be said to be in accord with the way.

However, whether in relation to one's employer—which goes without saying—or in relation to one's parents, no upstanding warrior would ever be rude or remiss in their presence. When you still are not at all negligent even when out of sight, where your employers and parents don't know what you are doing, and your conduct in the dark of night is no different from that in the light of day, this is called the loyalty and familial duty of warriors.

Wherever you sleep, don't point your feet in the direction of your employer. Where you set up straw bundles for archery practice, don't let the arrows land in the vicinity of your employer, and when you set your spear and sword on their racks, don't point the tips toward him.

In addition, sit up straight whenever you hear something or say something relevant to your employer. It bodes ill to lie around in a slovenly manner gossiping about your employer, or to read a letter from your parents too casually, throwing it away afterwards or tearing it up to make pipe cleaners or lamp cleaners.

When people with attitudes like this meet members of other establishments in other places, they hold forth on the negative aspects of their own employers' establishments. Or if they meet someone who sweet-talks them, they gladly spread bad rumors about their parents and siblings, ridiculing and slandering them. Because of this, some day they will be punished by their employers or parents, or meet with a serious calamity, or die the death of a warrior abandoned by fate; even if they survive, they will be good for nothing, or at any rate will never lead a decent life.

During the Keichō era (1596 1615) there was a courageous knight named Kani Saizō, who was the commander of the infantry under Fukushima Masanori, Grandee of the Imperial Guard of the Left. He was keeper of the Iron Gate of the castle of Hiroshima in Aki. As he kept watch day and night, because he was very old he used to take naps to rest.

Once an acolyte in Masanori's personal service came

to Saizō while he was napping, bringing a quail caught by a falcon. The acolyte reported that the quail had been sent to Saizō by Lord Masanori, whose falcon had caught it.

Hearing this, Saizō got right up, put back on the formal outer wear he had doffed for his nap, and faced the direction of headquarters to receive the gift, saying he would immediately go there to express his thanks. Then he scolded the acolyte, "Even though you're just a boy, you're a real moron! If it's a message from the lord, first you should announce that fact, wait for me to get ready, and then deliver the message. Instead you had the nerve to give me a message from the lord while I was still lying down! If you were not a mere boy you would be punished for this, but seeing as how you're only a child I'll let you go."

Shaken up, the acolyte hurried back and told the page boys what had happened. Masanori heard, and called that acolyte to him and asked him about it. The acolyte told the whole story. It is reported that Masanori said, "It was reasonable for Saizō to get angry at your impoliteness. I wish all the warriors of the provinces of Aki and Bizen had Saizō's heart. Then anything could be possible."

Horsemanship

I N OLDEN TIMES, THEY say, warriors of all ranks considered archery and horsemanship the highest martial arts. Warriors of recent times concentrate on practicing swordsmanship, lancing, and horsemanship as essentials. As for other martial arts such as archery, shooting, sword quick-draw, and *jujitsu*, it is a matter of course for young warriors to practice them regularly mornings and evenings. When you get old, no matter what you want to learn, it doesn't go as you wish.

For warriors of lesser rank, it is particularly desirable that they learn to ride well, so that they can ride any horse, even rambunctious or unruly horses. Let me explain. Fine horses easy to ride are rare; even if they exist, they are the mounts of great warriors, not found tethered in the stables of warriors of lesser rank. But if you master horsemanship, you can spot a horse that is good but is too rambunctious, temperamental, or unruly, and buy it for a low price; thus you can always have a better horse than you could normally afford.

Generally speaking, judging a horse's color and coat is something warriors of higher rank do. For a warrior of lesser rank, it is reasonable not to reject a horse because of the color or coat; as long as it is a good mount, he realizes, it makes sense to acquire it.

A long time ago there was a warrior named Kakuganji, who worked for the establishment of the Murakami clan in Shin province; he was the commander of about three hundred horsemen, skilled archers among them. It was his practice to choose for his mounts horses that ordinary people generally rejected for bad coats. Instead of having his warriors practice on the training ground, he would lead them into the fields outside the castle, fifty or even a hundred horsemen at a time, Kakuganji himself in the lead. They would gallop this way and that over the plains, now seeming to fall off only to make a flying mount, now seeming mounted only to make a flying dismount, maneuvering so freely that they became famous as expert riders.

Because of this, in those days even the Takeda clan of Kai province was wary of an opponent as redoubtable as Kaku-ganji of Shin province. This was very much to Kakuganji's credit.

Generally speaking, according to tradition a war horse should be of slightly more than middling height in the middle, with a head of middling size, and hindquarters of middling size. For a warrior of lesser rank, however, who has no spare mount, it is desirable that his one horse have a large body and be tall in stature, with a head as high as can be, and hindquarters as broad as possible. But to want to deform the horse unnaturally, stretching the sinews of its legs to give it a longer stride, or cutting the tail sinew to prevent it from raising its tail, is an eccentricity that comes from ignorance of the way of warriors.

Let me explain. A horse with the tendons of its four legs stretched tires easily when going uphill, on a long journey, or when crossing rivers; so it becomes useless. A horse with a stretched tail sinew will slip its crupper when crossing a gully or a canal, and it is traditionally said that a horse with excessively broad hindquarters is unsuitable for riding on a narrow path.

There are two kinds of interest in horses, good and bad.

Ancient warriors' interest in horses was in their necessity for maneuvering while heavily armed. For them, horses were substitutes for their own two feet. What is more, depending on circumstances, their horses could also be wounded or killed. Even though horses are animals, they pitied them and always took care to feed and curry them attentively.

As for interest in horses these days, people think the idea is to buy intractable horses at bargain prices and retrain them, or pick out country-bred colts and train them, then wait for bidders, to sell them for high prices. This is the mentality of traders; it is worse than having no interest in horses at all.

Army Principles and Combat Principles

T HOSE WHO ARE supposed to be warriors, even if they are of low rank, should select an appropriate mentor from whom to receive instruction in the arts of war, gaining detailed understanding of army principles and combat principles, including the inner secrets.

Some may say it seems inappropriate for a warrior of lesser rank to make a show of army principles, but that is a very ill-considered view. Let me explain.

Throughout history, among the people who have been respected as the protectors of provinces and prefectures, or have gained fame as good generals, any number have risen from humble circumstances, without clan support, to accomplish great works. Even now, if you set out from the lesser ranks to establish yourself, it is not impossible to become even a regional commander.

Moreover, if they study military science, those who are originally intelligent will become even smarter, while those who are somewhat slow by nature will reach the point where they no longer say such stupid things. Therefore warriors should not fail to study military science.

However, if they cultivate the arts of war wrongly, they

get conceited about their knowledge, looking down on others around them. Spouting high-flown but untrue theories, they mislead the youth and spoil their dispositions. Although they speak words beyond their own capacity that may seem correct and true, in their hearts they are very greedy, always calculating gain and loss. Gradually their character degenerates, and there are those who even lose the mentality of warriorhood altogether. This is an error connected with the half-baked cultivation of military science.

If you are going to study military science, you should not stop halfway. You should practice until you reach the inner secrets, finally to return to original simplicity and live in peace. If, however, you spend your days in half-baked practice of military science, unable to reach the inner principles, thereby losing the way to return to original simplicity, thus remaining frustrated and demoralized, that is most regrettable.

In this context, returning to simplicity refers to a condition like your state of mind before having studied military science. Generally speaking, just as with bean paste that stinks of bean paste, since ancient times it has been traditionally said that when you meet a military scientist who stinks of military science, you cannot stand the smell.

PART
TWO

Managing the Home

Ⅰ F THE CONDUCT OF A warrior's wife displeases him in some way, he should explain the reason and admonish her in such a way that she will understand. If it is a minor matter, it is reasonable to forgive and set it aside tolerantly. However, if she has had a bad attitude all along and ultimately seems to be no good, he simply divorces her and sends her back to her parents. This is, however, an exceptional case.

Anyway, if you don't follow this advice but instead shout at your wife, who is to be honored as mistress of your house, abusing her with foul language, that may be the way of back-alley coolies of the business district, but it is certainly not appropriate to the behavior of a knightly warrior. How much the more objectionable it is to brandish your sword or punch her with your fist—this is unspeakable behavior, characteristic of a cowardly warrior.

Let me explain. A woman who was born in a warrior family and has reached marriageable age would never tolerate being punched if she were a man, but because of her low status as a woman she has no choice but to tearfully endure it. To abuse someone he sees cannot fight back is something a valiant warrior simply does not do. Someone who takes to what valiant warriors reject is called a coward.

Relatives

I N CONVENTIONAL USAGE, the sons of your older brothers and the sons of your younger brothers are both called your nephews. The sons of your sisters married into other families are also called your nephews. Yet to think of them as no different is characteristic of peasants and townspeople; it is otherwise with warriors.

For example, the son of your oldest brother who is the designated heir may be your nephew, but since he is to succeed your parents and elder brother, he is to be called the head of the house. Even though he is of a younger generation as your nephew, nonetheless, you treat him with the same respect with which you treat your parents and elder brother. You do not treat him as a nephew, but as if you were honoring the ancestors of the clan.

As for the second and third sons of your elder brother, as well as the children of your younger brothers, a conventional uncle-nephew relationship will do. In relation to the sons of your sisters, although they too are your nephews, since they have different family names it is reasonable to consciously be distant in your ordinary manner of speaking to them and in your manner of addressing them in letters.

Once you have sent your nephew, your younger brother, or even your son to another house for adoption, you should take that attitude. Whatever manner of language is used in private meetings and gatherings, when interacting with people of other houses and other places it is reasonable to be distant in manner.

If you want to treat your son or younger brother as if he were still your son or younger brother, even after you have made him the son of another house, you will not escape criticism from the relatives and retainers of his adoptive father. They will say that if you are going to take this attitude it would have been better to keep him with you.

If, however, the adoptive father has no close relatives, his house is not well run, and an adopted son hardly has any prospects of inheritance, then if he is your real son or younger brother it is hard to overlook this. In such a case it is reasonable to look after him, out of sheer necessity.

Next, suppose you marry off your daughter, and her husband dies after a son is born. Now your grandson is technically head of his household; in regard to the matters of succession, of whatever needs to be discussed with the late husband's relatives, eighty to ninety per cent should be left to their decision.

However, if the child becomes a ward of the relatives as an heir to an impoverished father, then since it is, after all, reasonable to look after your daughter in her hardship, you have to take care of both of them.

If the late husband's estate is sufficient, or if he had some savings, still it is expected that in-laws would not touch that. Even in the case of the grandson who is still a child, if you are going to look after him, in consultation with your daughter, if you do not get full consent, you are vulnerable to criticism from others.

Now suppose a family in the direct line of the head of your clan, or in the direct line of your ancestors, or among your standard bearers, should suffer a decline and fall in the world. Your proper attitude as a knight is not to distance yourself from them, but to keep up good relations and ask after them from time to time. To be an opportunist and a fair-weather friend, honoring the unworthy when you see them thriving and despising the worthy when you see them in decline, is the mentality of peasants and merchants; it is not right for a warrior.

Frugality

WARRIORS IN PUBLIC service, whether of great or small status, should always be frugal and careful not to overspend.

In the case of salaried knights, however, even if they go broke at some point, if they quickly change their thinking and economize wherever they can, fastidiously simplifying their affairs, before long they can restore their finances. This is because they have a surplus.

If those of lesser rank imitate those of greater rank, overspending on useless things, since they do not have any surplus yet their cravings are unsatisfied, no matter how much they economize they cannot compensate. Eventually they will go broke, at a complete loss.

Individual livelihood is a private matter, but those who are in public service have to live up to the standards of their colleagues, so it is unavoidable to incur certain expenses. Under these conditions, if one is at a loss and therefore gets involved in all sorts of schemes, saying what should not be said and doing what should not be done, thereby getting a bad reputation, it is a mistake that ultimately arises from financial problems.

Therefore, fully aware of this to begin with, live within your means, taking care to avoid useless expenses, even minor ones, spending money only on imperative necessities. This is the way of frugality.

Yet there is something about frugality that must be understood. When you are obsessed with thrift, hate to spend money, and concentrate on skimping and saving, while you quickly restore your finances and become even more affluent than before, if you become acquisitive and miserly, eventually neglecting obligations and duties because all you are thinking of is saving up money, then this is being what is called a skinflint.

However it may be among peasants and townspeople, a knight who is a skinflint is much despised. That is because someone who disdains to spend money—which is abundant in the world—even for worthy purposes would certainly not freely give up his one and only life. Thus the ancients have said that a miser is another name for a coward.

House Building

WHEN A WARRIOR IN public service builds a house, it is reasonable if he makes its outward appearance — the gate, the guardhouse, the foyer, and the sitting room—as fine as is fitting for the warrior's status.

Let me explain. In any castle town, people from other places and other provinces can enter as far as the outer circle and look around. If the warriors' houses are nice and the homes appear peaceful, this would seem to be to the credit of the master of the castle as well.

Other than that, when it comes to the interior apartments for the wife and children and so on, it is reasonable to put up with whatever keeps out the rain, now matter how ugly it is, so as to spend as little as possible on the construction.

Let me explain. In times of warfare, even a great baron who is a master of a castle is always concerned about being surrounded and besieged in his citadel, so the houses of the warriors in the second and third circles are as a rule made low, narrow, and lightly constructed. Especially for the warriors of the outer circle, who all burn their own houses in a crisis, there is no way to build a house to be permanent. Therefore extremely light construction is described as like a shack to sleep in.

From this point of view, even in the present era of peace, knights who cultivate the way of the warrior should not construct fancy houses as if they were going to live there forever.

In case of a fire, moreover, it is necessary to set up a suitable shack right away. If you fail to take that into account and overspend on construction, willingly getting into debt, this can only be called eccentricity.

Military Equipment

KNIGHTS IN PUBLIC service must keep appropriate military equipment and weaponry corresponding to their status. This includes items that are in the military codes of every house and those ordained by their employers, such as the individual emblems, the helmet crests, the spear emblems, the sleeve emblems, and the carrier emblems—recognition emblems such as these must always be provided for the whole house.

If you try to provide these things suddenly in an emergency, your habitual neglect all along will be revealed, and there is no telling how people will look down on you. In ancient codes for warrior houses it says that those who are killed by their own allies because of neglecting recognition emblems have died for nothing. Thus there is no room for negligence.

For example, suppose you have your servants' sword blades made of wood or bamboo because you assume they are not going to have to kill anyone; or suppose there are the thoughtless who go around without loincloths because they assume they will not have to gird their loins, and you let them go on that way. This is inexcusable.

How much the more so for a knight in service. No matter how peaceful the times may be, if one is receiving a salary for military service yet does not consider the possibility of it, and fails to equip himself fully with necessary military equipment and weaponry, then he is a hundred times more negligent than those who fit swords with wood or bamboo blades or the youths and squires who don't wear loincloths.

Therefore you should conscientiously avoid negligence in the matter of military equipment. In this respect, there are some points to understand.

Suppose a warrior of lesser rank is going to get a full new outfit and intends, for example, to spend three pieces of gold on the whole set of gear. He should plan to spend two-thirds of that on the armor and helmet, and use the rest for underwear, pants, shirt, coat, chaps, battle jacket, whip, fan, mess kit, gear bag, canteen, and so on. It is essential to prepare all the necessary items as well as the armor.

Even if one is young and strong, furthermore, it makes sense to avoid heavy armor with thick metal, large banners, and large helmet crests. Armor made to match the strength of the prime of youth becomes useless when one gets older. Besides, no matter how young you are, if you are indisposed or wounded on the battlefield, even thin metal armor is sure to weigh you down and tire you out. This is why I say heavy armor is to be avoided.

As for large banners and large crests, when you have used them in every battle since youth and they are known to all the world, it is hard to put them aside just because they are burdensome when you get older.

Equipping Subordinates

A WARRIOR OF LESSER rank cannot command a large contingent of followers even in a time of emergency, so he cannot arm them with more than a spear. If that spear were to break, there would be a spear missing, so it makes sense to prepare a spare spearhead, fitting it to whatever shaft is handy at the moment, even be it a bamboo stick.

Also, supply long swords of sturdy make, even if somewhat damaged, for underlings to wield. Provide body armor with iron helmets for the young braves, breastplates, head cloths, and iron hats for the lackeys and squires; even if you are a warrior of lesser rank, you should be sure to outfit them with light body protection.

Furthermore, when there is a duel, since a sword may strike armor or helmet, it usually gets damaged. So it is essential to have a spare. Therefore when you take your subordinates along, it makes sense to have a squire carry your replacement sword, while the squire's sword is carried by a sandal bearer or groom.

Warriors

W ARRIORS ARE FUNC-tionaries who are sup-posed to punish criminals disrupting society, and bring security to the members of the other three classes. Therefore, even if you are of low rank, as a warrior you should not abuse or mistreat the other three classes.

To tax the farmers unreasonably and wear them out with all sorts of corveé labor, or to have artisans make things but not pay them for it, or to buy from merchants on credit and fail to settle accounts, or to borrow money and default on the loan—these are great injustices.

Understanding this, you should be sure to treat the farmers in your domain with compassion; see to it that the artisans are not ruined; and pay off loans to merchants, in small installments if lump-sum payment is impossible, so as not to cause them to suffer loss.

For a warrior whose duty it is to restrain brigandry, it will not do to act like a brigand yourself.

Modesty

U P UNTIL FIFTY OR sixty years ago, among the expressions relating to the careers of masterless warriors, to speak of "requiring at least a spare horse" meant requiring a salary of at least 500 koku of rice (one koku equals 5.119 bushels). To speak of requiring "at least an emaciated horse" meant requiring 300 koku without actually saying it in so many words. To "allow for wielding a rusty spear" meant hoping to get an office for 100 koku.

Up until those times, the ancient manners of warriors still survived, and these expressions came from unwillingness to voice specific figures. The saying that "a hawk, even if hungry, does not eat grain; a warrior, even if he hasn't eaten, sports a toothpick" was a proverb of those times. Young people did not talk about things like incomes and the prices of commodities, and they would have blushed on hearing talk about sex.

For those who are supposed to be warriors, it is desirable to try to emulate the manners of the old-fashioned warriors, even if they cannot fully attain them. If you take the attitude that "even if the nose is crooked, as long as you can breathe through it, that's good enough," there's no use saying any more.

Choosing Friends

A WARRIOR IN PUBLIC service may have many colleagues, but it is natural to develop friendships with warriors who are brave, just, intelligent, and influential. There are not so many warriors like that, so if there is even one who also associates with your other friends, he can be a big help in a time of need.

Generally speaking, it is inappropriate for warriors to fail to be selective about their friendships, becoming familiar with anyone at all, drinking and dining together, exchanging frequent visits. Let me explain.

Warriors can become close friends only when they see into each other's hearts. Warriors are not to associate casually just for a good time or a congenial conversation. If they totally lose their sense of decorum, behaving familiarly, passing nights singing, if they should feel they are on such good terms that they get to talk carelessly, they may wind up alienated, no longer speaking. With no one to reconcile them, they may eventually shrug it off, without the pride to set things straight. Their outer appearance may be that of warriors, but their psychology is that of common laborers. One should beware of this.

Friendly Relations

FOR A WARRIOR TO take pride in being dependable is correct according to the chivalric code. Nevertheless, if you make a show of dependability for no good reason, showing up where you have no business, taking on burdens you shouldn't trouble yourself with, then you are called a meddler, a busybody; this is not good at all. Even if it is some matter you think you might take some interest in, if you are not asked it is best not to get involved.

Let me explain. If you are a warrior, once you have accepted a request for a favor you have to take it upon yourself to do it, no matter how difficult it may be. Depending on how things go, it is not impossible that you may have to sacrifice your very life for your employer, your parents, or your brothers. That is why I advise against making a show of dependability without a good reason.

When ancient warriors were asked for something, they would consider its feasibility, and if they thought it unfeasible, they would not agree to it to begin with. Even something they thought feasible they would agree to undertake only after careful consideration; therefore, anything they had actually agreed to would be taken care of without fail.

For that, one would even be praised as a troubleshooter.

If, however, you readily assent to anything people ask, without due consideration, and you think nothing of it when it doesn't work out, you will get to be known as a good-for-nothing.

Now then, expressing your opinions to others, or objecting to their views, are also things that should be done with due consideration. Although it does not matter very much if people express their opinions too much, whatever they may be, when talking to their parents, teachers, brothers, uncles, children, students, or nephews, nevertheless anything a warrior says must be tactful and considerate. How much the more so when speaking with friends and colleagues; tact is even more appropriate under those circumstances.

Then again, if someone comes to you for advice, to absolutely refuse on the grounds that it is beyond you too is an exceptional case. Once you have become someone's confidant, it shows a certain degree of dependability to pursue the truth and speak your mind freely even if the other person doesn't like what you say.

If, however, you are fainthearted and fear to speak the truth, lest you cause offense or upset, and thus say whatever is convenient instead of what is right, thereby inducing other people to say things they shouldn't, or causing them to blunder to their own disadvantage, then you are useless as an advisor.

Then again, if there are those who are so lacking in intelligence that they reject advice, and make mistakes because of self-important heedlessness, insisting on doing things their own way, you cannot keep friendly relations with them.

Severing Relations

Awarrior in public service may have among his colleagues someone with whom he has severed social relations for some reason. In a case where their employer has ordered them to work together, he should go directly to the other party and say, "I have been appointed to work in the same office with you, and I have accepted the appointment. Although I no longer have social relations with you, now that we have been assigned to the same office let us consult freely with one another so that official business may go on without hindrance.

"Since you are my predecessor and senior colleague in this office, I solicit your guidance in all matters. However, if you and I should be assigned to different offices tomorrow and cease to be coworkers, then we will again have nothing to do with each other. Until that time, let there be only unhindered communication."

To make this clear and work together cooperatively is the right thing for a warrior to do. It is even more so in the case of colleagues with whom you have no problems—if you are working in the same office, you should be able to consult together freely.

Now then, suppose one lacks the kindness to see to it that an inexperienced newcomer manages to do his job, and one delights in seeing him make mistakes. This is nasty and vile—no, it is unspeakable. Warriors with a mentality like that are sure to do something cowardly in times of crisis, like stealing others' battle trophies for their own credit, or killing men on their own side. This is something of which to be conscientiously wary.

Fame

AWARRIOR OUGHT TO read ancient records regularly in order to steel himself. In famous books such as *Kōyō Gunkan, Nobunaga-ki, Taikō-ki,* and so on, and in records of battles, the names of those who did distinguished deeds are mentioned, and also the total numbers of deaths are recorded. Among so many thousands or hundreds of deaths, there must have been many who were knights of major status whose names were not recorded because they did not do anything special to merit it. Warriors of distinguished military achievement alone have their names recorded, even if they are of minor status.

For those who died ignominiously and those who died gloriously, the pain when they handed their heads to the enemy was no different. Realizing this, the true attitude of a warrior is to determine that if you are going to have to give up your life anyway, you may as well die heroically, startling enemies and allies alike, regretted by employers and commanders, an honor to your posterity for all time.

In contrast, to lag behind the others when attacking, yet to make sure to be the first in retreat, or to crouch behind one's comrades in the thick of fire when besieging an enemy castle, using them as a shield, and then to be downed by a chance arrow, trampled underfoot by your own allies, dying a dog's death, losing life, the most precious thing of all—this is the most bitter mortification, a regrettable situation; for a warrior no indiscretion could be worse.

Contemplate this point well, and strive to ponder it and practice it day and night.

Big Talk and Criticism

AMONG WARRIORS THERE are those who talk big and those who criticize; they seem similar, but it should be understood that they are very different.

Let me explain. Among warriors of old there were any number of knights who had gained a reputation for big talk. Even among the bannermen of the shogun there have been some big talkers. In their time, there were a handful of warriors known as big talkers in the establishment of the baronial houses in every province.

Those big talkers had all done distinguished military service time and again, and lacked nothing in terms of the warrior code; yet they were held back socially and professionally by the fact that they could sometimes be so stubborn that they could not serve as advisors. Their salaries and positions did not match up to their distinguished reputations, so they developed a devil-may-care attitude, saying whatever they wanted to, whenever they wished. And yet the overlords and their top councillors ignored them as beyond the pale, so they became more and more uninhibited, declaring people's virtues and vices without reserve or apology, big talkers for the rest of their lives.

As for the big talkers of today, they have never even donned a suit of armor, yet whenever they get together with their cronies they criticize their employer's management of the establishment, or the personnel policies of the board of directors; and besides that, they also gossip to their hearts' content about their peers and colleagues. People like this, morons who think they alone are the smart ones, are vastly different from the big talkers of ancient times. What they do should rather be called bad-mouthing, or talking trash.

Travel

When KNIGHTS IN public service travel, those of low rank may have to ride on packhorses. In that case, they should secure their long and short swords, to be sure that they don't come out of their scabbards in the event of a fall from a horse. Even so, you should not wrap the hilts in towels or something like that to keep them secure. The same applies to tying up a spear sheath with rope to keep it on. These are not merely matters of individual carelessness— the baggage is marked, identifying your employer's name, so the very manners and norms of your employer's institution will thereby appear to be weak.

Now then, these days there is a custom of changing horses through the offices of hostlers. If the rider before you is a knight, wait until you have seen him dismount at the hostler's bidding; then you can also dismount. The reason for this is that if you dismount as the hostler says and stand there waiting, if the previous rider says he won't change mounts you cannot insist on changing. Then even though you have already dismounted, you will have to remount the same horse in deference to the other man.

On the road, at fordable rivers be sure to hire carriers to take you across. If you cross by yourself to avoid a little expense, or because you think you are an expert in the water, and then the horse stumbles and the baggage gets soaked, or you get an underling injured, that is a big blunder.

As for those who board the ferry at Yokkaichi or take a boat at Awazu thinking to take a shortcut, they are extremely foolish. If you run into a squall while riding on the boats of Kuwana, the way everybody goes, then you have an excuse. But if you go to trouble on your own initiative to take a byway and something goes wrong, then you have no excuse.

Therefore a poem by an ancient says,

Even if crossing Arrow Bridge
Is a shortcut for a warrior,
If you're in a hurry take the roundabout way—
The long bridge of Seta.

This instruction does not apply only to a journey; one should have this attitude in regard to all things.

Warning Against Backbiting

FOR A KNIGHT EMPLOYED in public service, it is essential to always be careful not to gossip, even if you see or hear bad things about your colleagues.

The reason for this is that you never know what kind of mistakes or misunderstandings you yourself may make. Furthermore, the senior executives and officers are appointed by the overlord who employs you, according to his perceptivity; so to speak ill of them is tantamount to slandering your employer.

Furthermore, it may happen that for some reason you may need to ask those people for something, and be constrained to watch for when they are in a good mood and beg with palms joined and knees bent, silencing the mouth that up till now was slandering and criticizing. Regardless of what the matter is, this is not the sort of talk that should come from the mouth of one who is supposed to be a warrior.

Guardianship

DURING THE ERA OF Warring States, if a knight fell in battle after putting up a good fight, or if he was mortally wounded and eventually died, out of particular consideration the overlord or commander would allow that knight's son—if he had one, that is—to inherit his position without contest, even if the boy had only been born that very year.

Even so, since the child was too young for military action, if his father's younger brother was not in service he might be appointed by the overlord to succeed his older brother temporarily and look after the young heir during his minority. This was called guardianship.

There is an ancient code for guardianship. If you succeed your elder brother under the aforementioned circumstances, it is a matter of course to think of your nephew as your own son and bring him up with genuine compassion.

Now then, if you succeed your elder brother, it is essential to gather all the military gear, equipment for the horses, and other miscellaneous paraphernalia, and make a detailed examination and written inventory of all of it within the family, in the presence of one or two others.

When the boy reaches the age of fifteen, you should write a letter requesting that the position you have been holding be turned over to him, and that he be allowed to go into service the following year when he turns sixteen and can assume the duties of knighthood, young though he may be.

At that point, depending on rank, it is not impossible that you may be told that your request is acceptable but that you should continue on the job for two or three more years because your nephew is still a youth. No matter how pressing the insistence, refuse; then when your request is granted, hand over all the late father's effects, according to the inventory made at the outset of your guardianship. If there are any articles acquired during your guardianship that ought to be handed over, keep a record of them and pass them on too.

Now then, if, as mentioned, you are told to stay on as head of the family, it may be suggested that of an original salary of 500 koku, 300 be given to your nephew while you take 200 yourself if you maintain guardianship for a few years. In that case, express gratitude, but also express concern that the emolument of the main house would be reduced. You should request that the full amount of your late elder brother's stipend go to your nephew, while you yourself retire.

It should be the aim of a knight serving as a guardian to be as described above. In contrast, to refuse to cede family headship to your nephew when he comes of age to start military service, or even if you do cede it, to lose the family heirlooms during conservatorship, to leave the house in a shambles without making repairs, to pass on loans and debts your brother had not left, and even importune your young nephew for food and money, may be said to be most unprincipled.

Facing Death

THE FOREMOST CONCERN of a warrior, no matter what his rank, is how he will behave at the moment of his death. No matter how eloquent and intelligent you may normally seem to be, if you lose composure on the brink of death and die in an unseemly manner, your previous good conduct will all be in vain, and you will be looked down upon by serious people. This is a very disgraceful thing.

A warrior performs distinguished military feats on the battleground and earns the highest honor only after having accepted the fact that he is going to die. Because of that, if he has the misfortune to lose in a duel, when his head is about to be taken by the enemy, on being asked his name by the enemy he identifies himself clearly and hands over his head with a smile, showing no sign of flinching.

Alternately, if you are wounded so badly that surgeons cannot help, the right thing to do as a warrior is to speak to your officers and comrades clearly and take care of your wounds as long as you remain conscious, passing away calmly.

Considering death in this light, even if it is a time of peace, even a young warrior, to say nothing of an old one, should prepare himself mentally in case of a major illness, seeing to it that he can leave this life without regret. This applies if he is a major official, of course, but even if he is a minor functionary he should invite his superior over while he can still talk, offer his thanks and apologies, and announce his impending death.

After having done that, he should also bid a final farewell to his family and friends, calling his children to him and telling them, "To die of illness even though long patronized by an overlord is not the real aim of a warrior, but it cannot be helped. While you are young, carry on my will; and if there is a natural reason, by all means be prepared to serve the overlord, always being loyal and dutiful, working hard in public service. If you violate this covenant and act disloyally or unjustly, be sure I will disown you, even though I am under the shadows of leaves of grass."

To make a definitive final statement is a duty of a true warrior. Even as a sage, it seems, has said, "When people are about to die, let their words be good."

What is described above may properly be called the way a warrior dies. In contrast to this, if you fight death, refusing to consider an illness fatal, delighting when someone minimizes your illness and hating when someone says it is serious, fussing with doctors, making impossible prayers and vows, thinking in a confused manner, making no final statement even though your illness gradually worsens, this is like the death of a dog or cat. To spoil your one and only last hour like this is a slovenly way to die, resulting from failure to keep death in mind at all times—as recommended in the beginning of this book—hating to hear when someone dies, feeling that you will be in this world forever, being deeply desirous and greedy for life. If you go onto a battlefield with such a cowardly attitude, there is no way you can die a splendid death in the cause of loyalty and duty.

This is why those who cultivate warriorship refer even to dying in bed of sickness as the "once-in-a-lifetime major event."

PART THREE

Service

WHEN YOU ARE A knight in service, if your overlord is in financial straits because of major expenses, he may have no choice but to ask you for a loan from your regular salary for some years. Regardless of the amount, great or small, once you have agreed it is not the attitude of a warrior to complain to anyone about what hardship and trouble it is, even in casual conversation with your wife and children.

Let me explain. From olden times, and even now, it has been an established rule of warrior houses for vassals to get together and help out when their overlord is in difficulty, and for an overlord to use his power to help out vassals in difficulties. When an overlord has financial troubles, this affects the public domains. Even things an overlord is supposed to do, as proper to the baronial office, are generally canceled; for the vassals, it is distressing and dismaying to see their overlord barely able to make do.

Ordinary life goes on, but when there is an unexpected border disturbance—as may happen any day—and orders come down to go there on standard military service, when it comes to making preparations the first thing needed is money. When a young overlord is stuck and has no way to raise money no matter how clever he is, and meanwhile the other barons are making preparations for imminent deployment on a fixed date, even if your contingent is poorly prepared you have to show up.

In a time of peace, a martial procession before the eyes of all classes is considered a fine spectacle. Since it is a show, if the trappings of the men and horses of your establishment are inferior to the others, that would be unseemly, so it would be the disgrace of a lifetime for the overlord and commander. Considering how serious this can be, the knights of the establishment, both major and minor, newcomers and old-timers alike, are obliged to give up part of their salaries, according to their means.

Therefore, during the period of years when your income is reduced, you must be thoughtful about economizing in every way, reducing the numbers of personnel and horses, wearing paper and cotton clothing in winter and hemp clothing in summer, eating unpolished rice and miso soup with bran morning and night. Draw the water and split the firewood yourself; have your wife do the cooking. Endure the hardship to the best of your ability, focusing on the intention to set the overlord's finances in order somehow; this should be the fundamental motivation of service.

Furthermore, during that period of hardship, it may happen that you are given special duties and therefore have emergency expenses for supplies. You should meet those expenses yourself, without asking to borrow money, even if you have to pawn your spare sword and your wife's jewelry box. This is taking care to prevent others from talking, because even if the overlord doesn't hear of it, the senior officials of the establishment may look down on you, thinking that you are being importunate in a manner unbecoming to a knight because you have had your salary reduced.

Vassalage

A<small>WARRIOR WHO ACCEPTS</small>
a salary from an overlord
for service as a knight cannot fulfill his duties as long as he
considers his body and life to be his own.

Let me explain. There are two levels of people in service in warrior houses. The low-ranking lackeys and squires are busy day and night, and they work hard, but there is no convention that they have to sacrifice their very lives for the interests of the overlord. Therefore if they act irresolutely on the battlefield, there is no particular opprobrium attached to that in their case. So they can be called employees who sell only their bodies.

A knight, in contrast, has devoted his very life to service. Because lordship is originally a military office, in case of emergencies a lord is supposed to provide a militia corresponding to his status.

For example, a lord with a fief of 100,000 koku is officially supposed to provide a militia of 170 horsemen, 60 infantry archers, 350 infantry gunners, 150 lancers, and 20 bannermen. The number of extra personnel brought along in addition to the official requirement depends on the capacity and will of the commander.

Now then, when a militia like that is led out onto the

battlefield, enough men must be left behind to secure the castle and defend it from siege. Therefore, even though so many are not always needed, a large number of warriors are maintained. Among the many warriors of an establishment, there may be some born with physical handicaps, or some who seem to lack determination, but they are looked upon with tolerance and allowed their hereditary commissions.

Therefore, as a vassal, one should acknowledge the special relationship with one's overlord alone out of all the provincial lords and local lords in Japan. Even if you have a small stipend of 100 koku, in ten years that makes 1000 koku of rice. So if you collected all the rice your family has received in the decades from the times of your ancestors until your own time, how much would that amount to?

When it comes to requiting this favor from your overlord, if you just perform ordinary duties as guard, escort, or emissary—jobs known as hanging around doing nothing in peacetime—that is common mediocrity; it can hardly be called outstanding service.

But any day there may be an emergency; the essence of knightly service is to make up your mind privately, calling the God of War to witness, that you will not have others do what you should do yourself, be it leading a charge as first lancer, or leading a siege as first charioteer, or leading the rearguard in retreat when your side suffers a reverse, or, depending on rank, standing up to a barrage of enemy arrows in place of your lord and commander, or standing firm to die a heroic death in battle.

Regardless, once you have mastered this essence, your body and your life are not your own. Since you never know when your overlord may need you, you take care of yourself more fastidiously, avoiding unhealthy habits such as overeating, heavy drinking, and sexual promiscuity. Do not consider it a proper aim to die at home in bed, let alone by starting a quarrel in which you kill your comrades and lose your own life—you should abandon this sort of disloyal and irresponsible behavior.

To avoid this, it is best not to speak thoughtlessly. Arguments come from speaking out, and once an argument arises, there is inevitably offensive language. When two warriors get to the point of exchanging offensive language with each other, there is no way it can end without incident.

Therefore the loyal and dutiful knight, or the one who may be said to be intelligent, is the one who realizes this and restrains himself and refrains from involvement at the very outset of an argument, reminding himself that he has already devoted his body and life to his overlord.

Military Service

G ENERALLY SPEAKING, the official duties of warriors are twofold: combat and construction.

When the world is at war, day in and day out there is a battle here, a skirmish there—a warrior cannot rest easy for even a day.

Construction goes along with military operations—a stronghold here, a moat there, a barricade, a fort, an outpost. The backbreaking labor of all ranks on a rush construction job, which may continue day and night, is strenuous indeed.

In times of peace there is no combat, so there is no construction for that purpose. Therefore the knights under a military commander, both great and small, are assigned various duties such as guard, escort, emissary, and so on.

If people think that these civil duties are the real work of a knight, they do not call to mind combat and construction, the essential duties of warriors. When assistance for a public project is demanded of the barons by the shogun, even on rare occasions, and the expense, being large, is distributed among the knights of their establishments, so each can chip in a little, resentment and grumbling over this as an unwarranted expense ultimately come from ignorance of the fact that combat and construction are the essential duties of knighthood.

Now when it comes to ordinary duties such as guard, escort, or emissary, if you think it terribly troublesome to do your everyday job, and you feign illness to pass the work on to your colleagues without giving it a second thought; or in case of an emissarial duty, where you have to travel, if you are reluctant to get your travel expenses together and suffer the hardships of the road, and so you feign illness to leave the expense and bother to others, undaunted by the contempt of your colleagues; or even if your mission is to somewhere nearby, if you indulge in useless grumbling within earshot of colleagues about having to go out twice in one day or about going out in the rain, doing the job with a bad attitude even as you toil, then you are like a lackey or a squire wearing the skin of a knight.

When knights born in the Era of Warring States went to battle, in summer the blazing sun beat down on them in their armor, in winter the cold wind blew right through their armor. They were drenched by the rain, covered by the snow. In the fields and mountains they slept pillowed on the sleeves of their armor, and they had only unpolished rice and salt soup to eat. Whether in open combat, in besieging castles, or in defending citadels, they suffered and toiled; the only thing they didn't experience was simple normality.

When we think about it from this point of view, it is very lucky to happen to be born in an era of peace, when we hang mosquito nets in summer, wrap ourselves in nightclothes and quilts, eat what we like morning and night, and live in peace and comfort. So there is no good reason to think of domestic guard duty or local escort or emissarial duties as troublesome hardships.

It is related that a famous warrior known as the Master Archer used to have a sign on his wall with four words he applied in everyday life: "Always on the Battlefield." I note this for the edification of novice warriors.

Discretion

I F SOMEONE IS PRESENTED with a jacket or suit bearing his overlord's crest, when he wears the jacket he should wear a suit with his own crest on it; and when he wears the suit with his overlord's crest, he should wear a jacket with his own crest. It would be discourteous to his overlord if he were to wear both jacket and suit with his overlord's crest at the same time, because that is the way the overlord's relatives dress.

When the jacket or suit one has received has become too old to wear, the overlord's crests should be cut out, and they should be incinerated. That is to avoid soiling the over-lord's emblems.

Now then, when there is a serious illness or a tragic event in the home of a colleague in the neighborhood, even if you are not on familiar terms with him you should carefully avoid loud laughter, singing, and such things. You should also instruct your wife, children, and servants to do likewise. This is not just because of what that particular person may think; it is a matter of discretion, being ashamed to be held in contempt by your peers as an inconsiderate and unmannerly individual.

Verbal Expression

WHEN A KNIGHT IN service is given the important job of execution at large by his overlord, he should be sure to say, "For me to have been appointed to this official task, out of all the many men of the establishment, is a fitting fate for a warrior, for which I am grateful; of course I will accept without reluctance." A lukewarm acceptance, in contrast, is no good at all.

Let me explain. Even if you are bravely determined to carry out the execution in a laudable manner for your overlord, since victory in a duel depends partly on luck you may fail to accomplish the execution and even be killed yourself in the process, when the man you are sent out to execute at large fights back. In any case your colleagues will judge you afterward, for better or worse.

If things turn out well, people will praise you, saying that even though you looked able to get the job done from the moment you accepted it, still you did it remarkably well. Or if you failed and were killed instead, people will mention how you took on the task and will express their regrets, saying that you didn't seem as if you would be one to fail, wondering what went wrong.

Now then, if your acceptance was even slightly hesitant, even if you succeed well enough no one will praise you much; people will say it was luck. And if you fail, people will slander you, saying that your success was in doubt somehow from the moment you accepted—and after all you failed.

This is why acceptance must be done with good grace, without reluctance.

The foremost concern of all knights is never to blunder or slip up in any way on any account. For example, if you are importuned for help, think about it carefully, considering whether it is feasible or not. If you think it is unfeasible, that's another matter, but if you are ready to agree, then accept without any reluctance.

As in the aforementioned case, even if a request might be considered too much to ask, if you are reluctant and give the appearance of complying against your will, the other person will be especially dispirited and will think resentfully and bitterly that he would like to be able to avoid having to ask you, of all people, for a favor. To be like this is spineless and indecisive; it is a failure on top of a failure.

Family Histories

KNIGHTS IN SERVICE, even if newcomers, to say nothing of old-timers, should inquire of the elders so as to become knowledgeable about the origins of the overlord's house, his ancestors, his blood relatives, his affinal relatives, and even distinguished colleagues in the establishment unknown to the world at large.

The reason for this is that when you meet people of other establishments and converse with them, if you say you do not know or haven't heard, when you are asked about the house of your overlord, even though you may seem like a good worker on the whole, for this reason you will be thought of lightly.

Escort

WHEN A KNIGHT IN service accompanies his overlord on a journey, when they come to a way station he should talk to the local people, find out the cardinal directions in relation to mountains, woods, temples, or shrines visible nearby, find out what sort of open grounds there are in which direction from camp, and what the condition of the road is. It is essential to reconnoiter and make these determinations with certainty before the sun goes down. The reason for this is so that, in case a fire breaks out in the middle of the night and the overlord has to flee, the knight can take the lead and show the way.

Now then, when serving as a foot escort, be sure to go ahead of your overlord uphill and behind him downhill. This may seem trivial, but it is a part of service.

Use these examples as clues to think about what you can do to serve once you are in service. The basic intent of a knight should be to focus on this and work on it diligently day and night.

Officials

THERE IS A COMMON saying that white jackets and officials are best when new. Although this is a mere pleasantry, there seems to be some truth to it.

While a white jacket is new it is very nice, but when it has been worn for a long time it starts getting dirty around the collar and cuffs; before long, it becomes so gray that it is ugly and dirty.

This also applies to officials. While they are new on the job, they are innocent in every way, following the overlord's orders punctiliously, taking great care even with minor matters. In the process, they are conscientiously wary not to violate their oaths of office, so they do their tasks in a manner above reproach.

Yet even people who have thus earned the praise of their whole establishment as unselfish, upright, fine officials may in time become only superficially effective after they have worked at the job for a long time and learned all the ropes. Then they may make blunders they never would have made when they were new on the job.

Officials new on the job, furthermore, promptly return any gifts people give them, in accordance with their oath of office. Or if they have to accept a gift, they subsequently make a return gift of equal value. In any case, they do things cleanly. But even so, before they realize it, their sense of values has gone askew. As long as they are working this job they want to get something from it. They reason that if they promptly return a gift just because they have never accepted one before, they may not get another chance.

This ulterior motivation appears in their facial expressions and in the way they talk, and people are smart enough to get the idea. Outwardly they pretend to take no notice, but they manage to "donate" as much as they want through inside connections or other means. In return, they are able to skirt the authorities and get favored treatment. This corruption is equivalent to the sight of that white jacket turning ratty gray.

However, since the jacket is soiled by body oil, dirt, and dust, all you have to do is wash it with a good detergent and it comes clean. When the human heart is affected by all sorts of things that dirty it, in contrast, a simple wash and rinse, so to speak, will not get it clean. A white jacket, furthermore, only needs to be washed once or twice a year, but the human heart, even if cleaned constantly twenty-four hours a day, whatever you are doing, in all situations, still becomes dirty again easily.

There is a variety of detergents used for cleaning white jackets. Similarly, there are various practices that are like detergents for cleaning the hearts of warriors. What are these practices? They are loyalty, duty, and courage. There is dirt that is removed by the detergent of loyalty and fidelity, and there is dirt that is removed by the detergent of faithfulness to duty. When the stain remains stubborn even after washing with loyalty and rinsing with duty, then you use the detergent of courage, and make a determined effort to scrub it clean. This is the warrior's ultimate secret of cleaning the heart.

Borrowing Authority and Stealing Authority

For a knight in service, there is such a thing as borrowing the authority of the overlord, and there is such a thing as stealing the authority of the overlord. For an overlord too there is such a thing as lending authority to a retainer, and there is such a thing as having authority stolen by a retainer.

Suppose a knight who has been given an important job is young or low in status, depending on the customs of the establishment and the conditions of the times, he may have to work under the umbrella of the overlord's authority. Since it is for the overlord's sake to begin with, one temporarily borrows the overlord's authority to manage the business. This is called borrowing the authority of the overlord.

Having borrowed the authority of the overlord, when the knight has fulfilled the needs of the people and taken care of the overlord's business, he should then return that authority promptly and go about his work discreetly with the authority appropriate to his post. If, however, being treated with honor and having power behind him makes him greedy, eventually he winds up keeping the borrowed authority of the overlord. This is called stealing the overlord's authority.

Now then, for an overlord to lend authority to a retainer to bolster his power is an example set by many an enlightened leader and wise commander. This is called lending authority to a retainer. Trouble starts when the overlord does not reclaim his authority as soon as the task is done, instead leaving it lent out indefinitely. Eventually it becomes hard to retrieve; in effect, his authority has been usurped. This is called having authority stolen by a retainer.

This is not only a major personal and professional disgrace for an overlord, it is a source of many an injury and many a loss for him. If a retainer acquires too much influence, the overlord's authority and dignity will naturally be diluted. Everything will come to be up to the retainer, and all the knights of the establishment will take it that all you need is the agreement of that retainer to get official approval for things. The knights will therefore consider it essential to curry his favor, and will think little of the overlord.

Thus the lord and his following will become estranged, and so there will naturally be no way that loyal and dutiful knights can emerge in that establishment. Should an incident of upheaval happen to occur, there will be no good men to handle it.

Now then, when even the officers closely attached to the overlord, as well as the knights in civil offices, to say nothing of the knights in more peripheral positions, are all suppressed by the authority of that one man, and even though they know it is not good for the overlord, they all shrink from saying anything about it, none of them willing to come forth and let it be known to the overlord even though they resent it and in fact grumble about it in whispers to their intimate friends, then there is no way for the overlord to know about the man's arbitrariness, preferential treatments, and self-aggrandizement.

As a result of this ignorance, the overlord thinks whatever the man does is all right. The overlord will inevitably be criticized by society for getting himself into trouble by negligence and also by failure to size people up correctly—conduct unbecoming to someone in the position of an overlord and commander-in-chief.

On top of that, since this man does not fear even the eyes and ears of the overlord, much less take his colleagues' feelings or opinions into consideration, he will bribe the petty officials, use the overlord's supplies to give gifts to his cronies and take their return gifts for himself, and entertain guests with treats from the overlord's larder. Since he acts as if the overlord's things are his own, and his own things are his too, ultimately the overlord's finances are weakened. This is another one of the losses incurred by an overlord who lets his authority be usurped.

Understanding all this clearly, since we are granted the profoundly kind consideration of our overlord, it is essential that we be ever deferential, prudently restraining excessive pride and serving in such a way as to highlight the authority and dignity of the overlord in every respect. There is a reason for the old saying that "a loyal retainer knows he has an overlord; he doesn't know he has a self."

Exactions

FOR KNIGHTS IN PUBLIC service, the duties connected with the offices of the treasury are very difficult. That is because it is difficult for someone of ordinary intelligence and ability to meet the expenses of the overlord without causing hardship to the major and minor functionaries of the establishment, the townspeople living around the castle, and the farmers in the villages. When you think only of the overlord's interests, that becomes a hardship for those below, yet if you only try to please those below, the overlord's finances suffer. So either extreme presents a problem.

What is more, no matter how smart and talented a warrior may be by nature, his mind may easily become infected with the sickness of greed. So if one has a free hand in financing the overlord's expenses, providing for the personnel of the establishment, and managing the money, he may in time become conceited and wish to aggrandize himself. Then he cleverly embezzles from the overlord, builds a pretentious house, furnishes it with antiques, and entertains lavishly. Such a one is called a thieving minister.

Now then, suppose one formulates a new code, different from the measures of preceding generations, claiming that it is for the sake of the overlord, without admitting that it causes hardship for the whole establishment, imposing excessive duties on the townspeople, and burdening the village peasants with high taxes, perhaps interfering with future measures, giving no thought to whether or not it will affect the peasants badly, thinking only of immediate profit, duping less discerning elders and officers of the establishment to accept this, and obtaining unwarranted raises and awards through their offices. If the new code is unprofitable and ineffective, he will attribute it to the miscalculations of the aforementioned elders and officers, hiding in their shadow to avoid any blame, seeing to it that he suffers no inconvenience himself. Someone like this is called an extorting minister.

In the case of a thieving minister, even though he steals from his overlord and behaves in a manner unbecoming to a knight, when he is punished by heaven and is exposed, he loses his life. Once that individual falls, the problem is solved—he cannot cause others hardship and inconvenience any more, and he will no longer cause such impediment to the administration or trouble to the nation.

As for the extorting minister, he creates problems for everyone. Because he initiates irremediable policies that actually interfere with the government of the nation, even if he does not embezzle on his own account out of personal desire, nevertheless his crime is worse. That is why, in the words of the wise men of old, "It is better to have a thieving minister than an extorting minister."

For a knight, it may seem as though nothing could be

worse than getting the reputation of being a thieving minister, but as we understand the saying just cited, the ultimate crime lies with the extorting minister. Therefore, if the punishment for a thieving minister is decapitation, then the penalty for an extorting minister ought to be crucifixion.

However, it was precisely because in olden times extorting ministers and thieving ministers were distinct that they used to say a thieving minister is better than an extorting minister. In recent times, extorting ministers also act like thieving ministers, outwardly pretending to be looking after the interests of the lord while inwardly conniving to convert revenues to their personal use. They are extorting and thieving ministers all in one; they are bandits. What kind of punishment do criminals like this deserve? It is hard to tell.

Watch Commanders and Superintendents

K NIGHTS OF MINOR rank in service under watch commanders and superintendents realize that they must take personal responsibility for the moods of their superiors and the good and bad attributes of their group. If they themselves have the good fortune to become established as group leaders, they should properly treat each member of their groups sympathetically as they carry out their official duties. Of course, everyone realizes that there should be no partiality or favoritism at all.

As people gradually rise in the ranks to watch commander and superintendent, however, their attitude changes. There have been men who were quite good knights when they were of minor rank, but who became unreasonable when they reached major rank, so that they lost favor with their overlords and perished. I think these are useful examples of what can happen.

Laziness

As mentioned in the first chapter, for a knight who has an overlord, life is here today, uncertain tomorrow. Therefore he realizes every day that he has this one day to serve, so he does not become bored and does not neglect any of his duties. Because he does every task that very day, it stands to reason that he does not overlook anything or forget anything.

In contrast to this, when you think you will be on the job forever, then trouble starts. You get bored, so you become inattentive and lazy. You begin neglecting even urgent matters, to say nothing of less pressing affairs, putting them off to the next day or claiming that they've already been arranged, or fobbing them off on colleagues or flunkies. Since no one takes personal responsibility for taking care of them, tasks pile up and there is nothing but snafus. These are all mistakes that come from counting on having time in the future. You should be most wary of this.

For example, if you are assigned to a certain number of days a month on watch, you should be sure to figure the route from your home to your post, calculate how long it will take you to get there, and set out to be slightly early for the time of the changing of the guard. If you dawdle over tea, tobacco, and family talk, leaving home late for a post that you have to work in any event, suddenly you are in a blind rush, galloping to your post in a big sweat. Fanning yourself even in winter, you may try to quip that you were late because you had a little bit of a bothersome business. That is moronic. The watch duty of a warrior is security duty; no one should show up late for work for any personal reason whatsoever.

Now then, there are those who understand this much and so always show up for work early themselves, yet they become restless waiting for tardy colleagues, fidgeting and yawning, and hate to stay inside the governor's mansion even for a while, being in a hurry to go home. These are unseemly things of recent times.

Dealing with Emergencies

WHEN TWO OVERLORDS meet at a river crossing in the course of a journey, if their retainers get into a dispute and it blows up into a fight, then depending on how things go at the time, the overlords themselves might have to duel with each other. If two overlords get into a duel, there is no telling how it will all end.

Therefore it is essential to realize that "trouble arises from below," and to be careful when escorting your overlord on a journey. You must not only be alert yourself, but also alert your colleagues. It is essential to make sure to caution everyone down the line, even to the lowest ranks, not to do anything foolish.

Furthermore, when you are escorting your overlord in the capital city and you pass another overlord's entourage on the street, if the young braves in the vanguards of the two parties start disputing and get into a quarrel, take immediate notice, get our overlord's lance from the weapon bearer and bring it to the overlord's side. Watch how things go, and if it looks as if they are not going to settle down and the knights have all drawn their swords, bring your lord's horse to his palanquin, help him mount up, then unsheathe his lance and hand it to him. You too draw your sword and be prepared to act.

Now then, when you escort your overlord to a party, if something unexpected should happen during the festivities and it looks as if there is going to be a riot, go to the foyer with your sword in hand and announce to the receptionist, "I am so-and-so, retainer of so-and-so. It looks like there may be a riot here, and I am concerned about my lord. Please tell him I am here."

The receptionist may reply, "Although nothing serious has happened, your concern is reasonable. Your master is all right, so do not worry, and tell your colleagues too." In that case, first express gladness, but insist on having your lord called out so that you can see him with your own eyes before you withdraw.

Self-Expression

A S A KNIGHT IN SERVICE you may do such an extraordinary job for your overlord that you feel in your heart you have done a fine job, and others are also moved to praise you for it, yet the overlord does not seem to think so much of it. Or even if he does think so inwardly, outwardly there seems to be some reservation, for there is no particular reward forthcoming, and your effort seems to have been wasted. If you feel disgruntled and grumble about the ingratitude of the overlord, doing your job without enthusiasm, you have the wrong attitude.

The knights of the Warring States went into combat countless times throughout their lives, sacrificing their lives for their lords and commanders; they certainly would not do any boasting before they had attained great fame for their achievements. As for service in peaceful times, it's just a matter of how well you crawl around on *tatami* mats, rubbing your hands together, and dueling with your tongue—there is no such thing as fighting for your life.

Of course, when it comes to the attitudes of loyalty and duty, it makes no difference whether it is wartime or peacetime; these are official obligations of a knight in service. Whether that deserves any special reward as something extraordinary is entirely up to the overlord—all you have to do is be sure to do your own professional duty, and you have no reason to express dissatisfaction.

Dying Loyally

KNIGHTS IN SERVICE ARE so very favored by their overlord that there is no way for them to requite their debt. They may want to at least follow him in death by committing suicide when he dies, but this practice is no longer legal. Even so, it is mortifying for them to spend their whole lives indoors performing ordinary jobs.

If there is anyone who is determined to perform service beyond the capabilities of his colleagues, even at the cost of his life, that is a hundred times better than following the overlord in death. Not only is it good for the overlord, it is also a help to all the members of the establishment, great and small. Such a knight is of the highest grade, with everything needed to be an exemplar for latter-day warriors—loyalty, duty, and courage.

The house of a person of high status is invariably haunted by a vengeful ghost. There are two ways in which the vengeful ghost causes trouble.

First is the untimely death, through accident or illness, of a praiseworthy and promising young warrior from among the houses of hereditary elders and seniors of the establishment, one with all three knightly qualities of loyalty, duty, and courage, one who was certain to enter the service of the overlord and become a lasting credit to the house. This handicaps the lord.

Examples of this include the case of a great warrior commander who died young when he fell off his horse; this was said to be the work of a vengeful spirit that had long been haunting the house of his master.

The second way in which a vengeful spirit causes trouble is by taking over the mind of a knight who is especially liked by the overlord, then deluding the overlord and inducing him to do wrong.

Now then, there are generally six ways in which an attendant knight may delude his overlord.

One way is to contrive to block the ears and eyes of the overlord, so that neither the other officers nor anyone else can express their opinions; or, even if they can express them, he conveys them in such a way that the overlord will not take them seriously. Thus all the affairs of the establishment, great and small, go through this one man alone, making it seem to the overlord that he is indispensable.

The second way the knight may delude his overlord is to arrange for the transfer of any knights around the establishment who seem to have some mettle and who could be a help to the overlord. Distancing them from the overlord, the possessed knight installs only his own connections in offices close to the lord, sycophants and flatterers who will do as he says, seeing to it that the overlord never hears about his self-aggrandizement.

The third way the knight may delude his overlord is to

captivate the overlord's mind with women, claiming that it is good for alliances, and that there is nothing more important than having successors. The possessed knight gathers maids, without concern for their family backgrounds as long as they are pretty, and also musicians and dancers, persuading the overlord that he needs relaxation and recreation. Even a naturally intelligent lord is easily seduced by sexuality, to say nothing of a lord who is deficient by nature. Before long he becomes indiscreet and thinks it is fun to play. Inevitably this gradually intensifies, until eventually the overlord is partying day and night, staying in his seraglio and neglecting the affairs of his household and his domain. If other elders or seniors of the establishment want to meet with him, he is unwilling and leaves everything to that one individual, the knight who is possessed. As that one man manages things, his power grows day by day, so that the other elders and seniors of the establishment fade into obscure silence. Thus the modus operandi of the establishment becomes corrupted in all sorts of ways.

The fourth way the knight may delude his overlord takes place when many expenses are incurred secretly under the foregoing conditions, to the extent that there is no way to pay them off, and so new rules are created, contradictory to the measures of the previous generations. Here the possessed knight interferes in such a way as to withhold what is due to the members of the establishment, not recognizing the misery suffered by those of the lower echelons. Now since the overlord is spending all he wants on luxury, even if they do not say so openly the officers of the whole establishment, great and small, all feel discontent at heart, and so not one of them is genuinely loyal and dutiful.

The fifth way the knight may delude his overlord takes place when he himself does not care for martial arts in an auspicious era of peace such as this, and so in spite of the fact that there is no way an overlord could be personally unskilled in martial arts, he persuades the overlord that there is no need for military preparations. Those personnel of the establishment who are not trained to begin with consider that good and do not practice martial arts, or even equip themselves with armor and weaponry. Since they become accustomed to thinking that everything is fine as long as immediate needs are met, their establishment has none of the character of a house descended from a line of famous generals. If some incident should occur the next day, they will just run around in a panic, utterly ineffective, totally unreliable.

The sixth way the knight may delude his overlord happens when the overlord takes to carousing, drinking, and debauchery. As he gradually indulges more and more, even to the point of ruining his health, the knights of the establishment become demoralized and live each day as it comes, without any real sincerity. So public affairs and the fiats of the central government are not dealt with as they should be. Ultimately the status of the overlord may suffer, and that would be really bad luck.

Now even if the whole establishment hated the knight in question, who makes up the tax rolls, denouncing him as a devil in the house and an enemy of the overlord, with nine out of ten testifying to his iniquities, seeing no alternative but to take the matter to court and argue their case verbally without dirtying their hands, the problem would hardly be resolved privately—the overlord's whole organization could be investigated by the central government, and if things grew worse it could become a public scandal and a cause for government action.

Throughout history, there has never been a case where a baron who was unable to manage his establishment and therefore had to resort to the central government actually had the matter resolved that way and maintained his own position. Just as in the metaphors of killing an ox to straighten its horns, or burning down a shrine to catch a mouse, when the overlord loses his position the personnel of the whole establishment, major and minor, are all disenfranchised.

In this case, the logical thing to do is to seize the villain, that devil of the house, that enemy of the overlord, and do away with him as you will—run him through, or strike off his head—and then when that is done satisfactorily you immediately disembowel yourself, committing suicide. Then there will be no government inquiry, and the overlord's position will not be affected. Thus the personnel of the establishment will be secure, and the country will be peaceful.

In this way you become a role model for knights of latter days—loyal, dutiful, and courageous—a hundred times better than one who kills himself to follow his overlord in death.

Cultural Refinement

WHILE IT GOES WITHOUT saying that an attitude of hardness and strength is considered foremost in the way of the warrior, if strength is all you have you will seem like a peasant turned samurai, and that will never do. You should acquire education as a matter of course, and it is desirable to learn things such as poetry and the tea ceremony, little by little, in your spare time.

If you have no education, there is no way for you to understand the reasons of things past or present. Then no matter how smart or cunning you may be, in actual practice dealing with events you will run into many obstacles.

If you have a rough understanding of foreign countries and Japan, and you carefully consider the elements of time, place, and position in order to manage things according to what is appropriate, you will not make so many mistakes. That is why I say acquiring an education should be a matter of course.

However, if you develop the wrong attitude about education, it usually turns into conceit. You look down on the uneducated and illiterate, and on top of that you develop a bias for exotic things. You think anything that comes from abroad is good, insisting on your prejudices, and you do not recognize that such things are impractical in our country today, even if good in theory. This is a terrible state of affairs.

Now then, when it comes to the study of poetry, in accord with Japanese custom there have been famous generals and valiant knights throughout history who have mastered the art of composing poetry. So even if you are a warrior in minor rank, it is desirable to take an interest in poetry and even be able to compose the occasional verse.

Even so, if you cast everything else aside to concentrate solely on poetry, before you know it your heart and your face soften, and you get to look like an aristocratic samurai, losing the manner of a warrior. In particular, if you become too fond of this modern fashion of *haikai*, then even in the assemblies of reserved colleagues you may tend to come forth with puns, bon mots, and clever lines. It may be amusing at the time, but it is something to be avoided by someone who is a warrior.

As for the tea ceremony, it has been a pastime of knights since the era of the Kyoto Shoguns, so even if you do not take an interest in it yourself, nevertheless it may happen that you have to participate as a guest at someone's house, or as an escort to a noble of high rank. On such occasions, you have to know all sorts of things, such as how to approach and enter the tea room, how to look at the decor, how to eat, and how to drink tea. Therefore you should get some instruction in the tea ceremony and learn a little bit about it.

Regarding the tea room, furthermore, the point is to enjoy a realm of detachment and serenity apart from worldly wealth, status, and glory; thus, no matter how rich people are, or even if they are officials of the central government, in their yards they copy the scenery of the mountains, forests, streams, and valleys. With rafters of bamboo, pillars with the bark still on them, thatched eaves, exposed lath windows, bamboo blinds, crude doors, and gates of woven branches, a forlorn austerity in decor is considered fundamental. Even the tea utensils and furnishings are not supposed to be beautiful; the idea is to disdain the materialistic world and just enjoy pure, free naturalness. Thus it seems that this can be a help in mellowing the way of the warrior.

So even if you prepare a place for tea, it is not bad to enjoy simple, austere tea with a modern wall-hanging and utensils of recent manufacture.

Even so, in all things the light easily becomes heavy. Before you know it, you may develop a sense of luxury; seeing someone else with a fine teakettle, you become dissatisfied with your own. The same thing happens with all the other tea utensils too; gradually you come to want fine wares. Pretty soon you're looking for bargains, learning to appraise antiques and to get good utensils at low prices. You may see something nice at someone's house and keep asking him for it. And if you trade utensils you concentrate on getting the better end of the deal for yourself, your attitude becoming like that of a downtown merchant who talks about everything in terms of commerce. Thus you will lose the true meaning of the knighthood of the warrior's way, turning into a person of very bad character.

Rather than become a devotee of that kind, it is better to know nothing about tea at all. Even if you are so completely uncultivated that you don't even know how to drink this "ground tea" stuff, that doesn't hold you back on the warrior's way.

ABOUT TUTTLE
"Books to Span the East and West"

Our core mission at Tuttle Publishing is to create books which bring people together one page at a time. Tuttle was founded in 1832 in the small New England town of Rutland, Vermont (USA). Our fundamental values remain as strong today as they were then—to publish best-in-class books informing the English-speaking world about the countries and peoples of Asia. The world has become a smaller place today and Asia's economic, cultural and political influence has expanded, yet the need for meaningful dialogue and information about this diverse region has never been greater. Since 1948, Tuttle has been a leader in publishing books on the cultures, arts, cuisines, languages and literatures of Asia. Our authors and photographers have won numerous awards and Tuttle has published thousands of books on subjects ranging from martial arts to paper crafts. We welcome you to explore the wealth of information available on Asia at **www.tuttlepublishing.com**.

This edition published 2006 by Geddes & Grosset
New Lanark, Scotland.

© 1996 Geddes & Grosset

First printed 1996
Reprinted 1997 (twice), 1999, 2004, 2006

All rights reserved. No part of this publication may be
reproduced, stored in a retrieval system or transmitted, in
any form or by any means, electronic, mechanical,
photocopying, recording or otherwise, without the prior
written permission of the copyright holder.

ISBN 10: 1 85534 177 8
ISBN 13: 978 1 85534 177 7

Printed and bound in UAE

1 2 3

Judy Hamilton

Illustrated by Beverley Sprio

Tarantula Books

Counting at the farm is fun.
Let's begin; we start with **one**.
One tractor, **one** farmhouse,
One red front door...

Two green wellingtons, lying on the floor.
Two muddy footprints, one by each boot—
And **two** soggy socks, one for each foot!

Look inside and let us see
If we get to number three...

Three bright raincoats, hanging
on the wall;
Three boxes piled up—hope they
do not fall!
Three steps up to the kitchen to see...

Four chairs round the table, all set for tea.
How many plates? How many cups?
Count them and see!

Four panes of glass in the little back door;
Let's go out and see if we can count any
more...

Out in the garden, there's a little beehive;
Count the bees coming out—
One, two, three, four, **five**!

Right beside the beehive,
The farmyard gate of blue.
Count its **five** strong wooden bars
Before you step through...

Seven cows in the field,
Mooing as we pass.
Ssh! Count them quietly!
They're busy eating grass!

Let's go across the field,
Through another gate,
Keeping counting as we go,
For next comes...

Clucking round the farmyard,
A hen and her chicks;
Help the hen to count them—
Can you find **six**?

Washing blowing on the line,
Clean and nearly dry.
Try and count the **six** striped
sheets
As in the wind they fly.

7

Eight!

Beside the gate, along the fence
Are **eight** tall trees;
Count them all and listen to them
Rustle in the breeze.

Count the fence posts by the trees
Standing in a line;
One, two, three, four, five, six, seven, eight...

Then comes...

Nine!

Go back to the farmyard, along the lane,
And there, by the wall,
Stand **nine** shiny milk churns—
I wonder, are they full?

Up above the farmyard wall,
Swaying and swinging,
Nine birds sit on the telephone wire,
Cheerfully singing.

And in the barn, neatly stacked,
Are **ten** bales of hay.
Count the bales; then count the mice.
How many are at play?

Ten little flowers, growing in a line;
One flower wilted,
And then there were

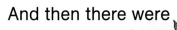

Nine little flowers, nodding, feeling great.
One blew over in the wind
So now there were

Eight little flowers, smiling up at heaven.
One shrivelled in the sun
And then there were

One little flower, sad and bereft;
Someone picked it for a vase...

Oh!...

...None left!

Four little flowers, then, oh, goodness me!
A rainstorm came!—washed one away!—
leaving only

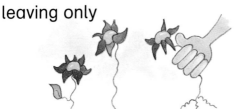

Three little flowers—oh, so few!
One was mistaken for a weed
So that left

Two little flowers, soaking up the sun.
One was eaten by a goat;
Now there was only

Seven little flowers, a colourful mix.
But a slug had one for dinner
And that left only

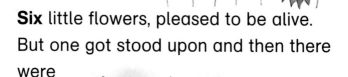

Six little flowers, pleased to be alive.
But one got stood upon and then there
were

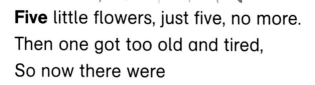

Five little flowers, just five, no more.
Then one got too old and tired,
So now there were